CELLS

CONSTRUCTING LIVING THINGS

Jodie Mangor

rourkeeducationalmedia.com

Before Reading:

Building Academic Vocabulary and Background Knowledge

Before reading a book, it is important to tap into what your child or students already know about the topic. This will help them develop their vocabulary, increase their reading comprehension, and make connections across the curriculum.

1. Look at the cover of the book. What will this book be about?
2. What do you already know about the topic?
3. Let's study the Table of Contents. What will you learn about in the book's chapters?
4. What would you like to learn about this topic? Do you think you might learn about it from this book? Why or why not?
5. Use a reading journal to write about your knowledge of this topic. Record what you already know about the topic and what you hope to learn about the topic.
6. Read the book.
7. In your reading journal, record what you learned about the topic and your response to the book.
8. After reading the book complete the activities below.

Content Area Vocabulary
Read the list. What do these words mean?

complex
diversity
energy
functions
gene
genetic information
microbes
micrometers
microscopy
nutrients
organism
photosynthesis
proteins
reproduce
scaffolding

After Reading:

Comprehension and Extension Activity

After reading the book, work on the following questions with your child or students in order to check their level of reading comprehension and content mastery.

1. How can you tell if something is alive? (Summarize)
2. What are some of the most important reasons to study cells? (Infer)
3. What is "Frankenmeat," and why would anyone eat it? (Asking questions)
4. How does medication affect the cells in your body? (Text to self connection)
5. How would our understanding of cells be different if tools such as microscopes didn't exist? (Asking questions)

Extension Activity

Make an edible plant or animal cell! With the help of an adult, bake a cake in a round pan according to the package instructions. After frosting the cake, use different-shaped candies to represent the cell's organelles.

Table of Contents

Life's Amazing Mini Machines 4

Inside Every Cell: A Cell's Inner Workings 8

Prokaryotes vs. Eukaryotes 15

Plant vs. Animal 22

Building with Cells/Cell Division 28

Building YOU 36

Tools of the Cell Trade 43

Glossary 46

Index...47

Show What You Know 47

Websites to Visit 47

About the Author 48

Life's Amazing Mini Machines

What do a tree and an elephant have in common?

A trunk!

Jokes aside, they are both made of cells. So is every other living thing, from the tiniest **microbes** to plants to humans, to the marvelously giant whale.

Cells are like tiny machines, carrying out all the work needed to keep us alive. They are the smallest units of life capable of reproducing themselves.

Is It Alive?!

How can you tell if something is alive? For something to be considered an organism, a living thing, it has to display every single trait on this checklist:

- It is made up of one or more cells
- It uses energy
- It maintains a steady, stable internal environment
- It grows
- It reproduces
- It is capable of detecting and responding to changes in its environment

What about viruses? Are they alive? The answer is no. While they carry all the information needed to make more of themselves, they can't **reproduce** on their own. Instead, they have to infect a cell and force its machinery to do the job.

Some organisms are unicellular, meaning they are made up of a single cell. Bacteria, yeast, and amoeba are all unicellular.

Other organisms are multicellular, with bodies made up of more than one cell, and sometimes trillions of cells.

Cells by the Numbers

How many cells does an organism have?

- Lactobaccillus (a bacteria used to make yogurt): 1 cell
- Simple roundworm: 1,000 cells
- Adult human: 37,000,000,000,000 (37 trillion) cells

Yogurt

Lactobaccillus

The **diversity** of cells is mind-blowing! They come in a huge array of sizes and shapes. These characteristics are influenced by where a cell lives and what work it needs to do to survive.

The human body has an estimated 37.2 trillion cells.

A fruit fly has 50,000 cells.

Cells of All Shapes and Sizes

Scientists recently discovered bacterial cells so tiny that 150,000 could fit into the tip of a human hair. Cells can also be huge. An ostrich egg (yes, it's a single cell!) is about the size of a melon and weighs over three pounds (1 kilogram), while a giraffe nerve cell can be several meters long.

A cell's size and shape can tell us a lot about what it does.

Unicellular organisms tend to be small. Their size allows them to take up **nutrients** and reproduce quickly, sometimes within minutes. These things help them to adapt to new environments.

In a single multicellular **organism**, there can be hundreds of cell types. Their many shapes and sizes help them carry out different life-supporting **functions** within that organism.

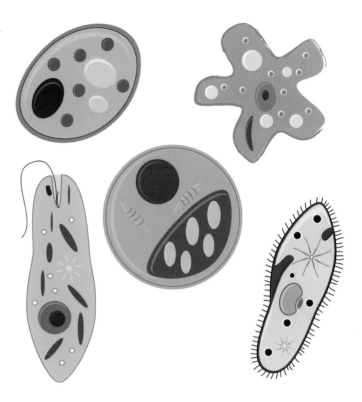

Cell Power

Nerve cells send signals from one part of the body to another. They have a long, thin shape with branches that reach out in different directions. This allows them to communicate with other cells quickly and efficiently.

Skin cells can be wide and flat, allowing fewer cells to cover a greater area. They are also packed tightly together. This allows them to form a smooth, strong, and stretchy barrier that protects the body from the outside environment.

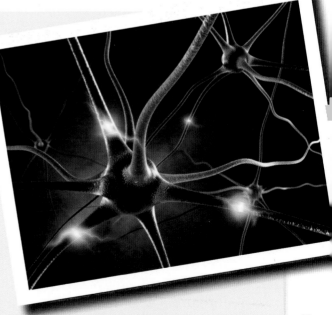

Inside Every Cell: A Cell's Inner Workings

For all their differences, cells have certain fundamental things in common. For starters, all living cells use **energy**.

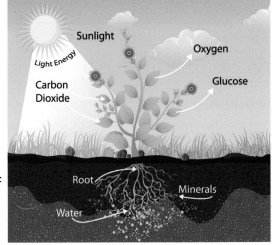

Energy gives cells the power they need to survive, grow, reproduce, and defend themselves. Without a source of energy, a cell will eventually die.

Where do cells get energy from? Some organisms, like plants, are producers. They create their own energy-containing food in a process called **photosynthesis**. Other organisms, like animals, are consumers. They get their energy by eating plants or other animals.

Reaction Action

Many chemical reactions go on inside a cell. Together, all of these reactions are called the cell's metabolism.

Anabolic reactions store energy by building complex molecules out of simpler substances. An example would be building carbohydrates out of simple sugar.

Catabolic reactions release energy for the cell to use, by breaking complex molecules down into simple substances. An example would be breaking a complex carbohydrate down into simple sugars.

All cells contain DNA, or deoxyribonucleic acid. Amazingly, all cells store their **genetic information** in the same way—encoded in DNA.

The DNA in each cell contains all the information needed to build an entire organism. It is like a master plan that tells a cell what to do, what to make, and when.

DNA Makes the Difference

When scientists compared the DNA in humans to the DNA in chimpanzees and gorillas, they found that we share approximately 99 percent of our DNA with chimpanzees and 98 percent with gorillas. The remaining one or two percent is enough to make us as different as we are.

What does DNA look like? A single DNA molecule is really two long strands that wrap around each other in a spiral called a double helix.

Different sections of DNA hold the instructions for different **proteins**. Each of these sections is called a **gene**. Genes hold hereditary information about things like our eye color, height, whether we have beaks or lips, fins or tails, or whether we walk on two legs or four.

Instructions contained in DNA can be copied multiple times, into molecules of RNA or ribonucleic acid. Each RNA molecule then provides the cell's machinery with instructions on how to assemble a particular protein.

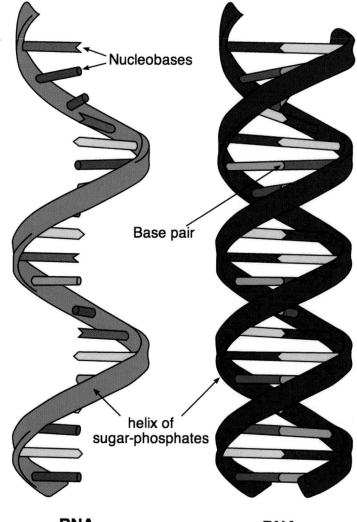

Nucleobases

Base pair

helix of sugar-phosphates

RNA
Ribonucleic acid

DNA
Deoxyribonucleic acid

Did You Know?

Complex organisms tend to have more DNA and more genes than simple organisms. Scientists estimate that humans have between 20,000 and 25,000 genes. A bacterium can have as few as 300 to 400 genes.

All cells have "machines" to make proteins. These machines are called ribosomes. To build a protein, a ribosome clamps onto a strand of RNA. The ribosome moves along the RNA, "reading" its instructions as it assembles the protein.

Proteins do many things in a cell. They give it its shape, control its behavior, and act as helpers to speed up chemical reactions.

Ribosomes are special because they are found in both prokaryotes and eukaryotes. While a nucleus is only found in eukaryotes, every cell needs ribosomes to manufacture proteins.

Ribosome

All cells are made from the same basic building blocks. Basic units of matter called atoms combine with other atoms to make molecules. Some of these molecules organize into organelles.

Organelles in a eukaryotic cell

Organelles are small structures that perform specific functions within cells, much like our organs perform specific functions within our bodies.

Sets of basic building blocks inside a cell and what they make:

- Nucleotides are used to make DNA. There are four different nucleotides: adenine (A), thymine (T), cytosine (C), and guanine (G). Just like letters of the alphabet can be combined in different ways to make words, nucleotides can be ordered to convey specific meanings.

- Amino acids are special molecules used to make proteins. Twenty different amino acids combine in many ways to make all the proteins in our bodies.

Each of these sets of building blocks can be arranged in an infinite number of ways, as illustrated in the 100 million or so species living here on Earth!

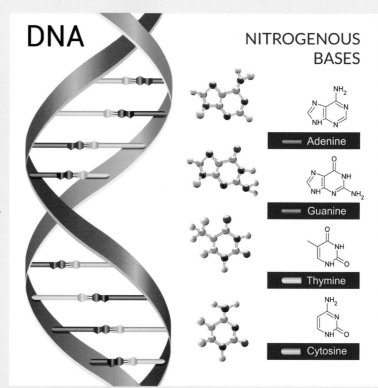

All cells have a plasma membrane. This membrane separates the inside of a cell from its surroundings. It acts like a gateway to the cell, letting some substances in and keeping others out.

All cells also contain cytoplasm, a jelly-like fluid of water, salts, and proteins. It fills all empty spaces within the cell.

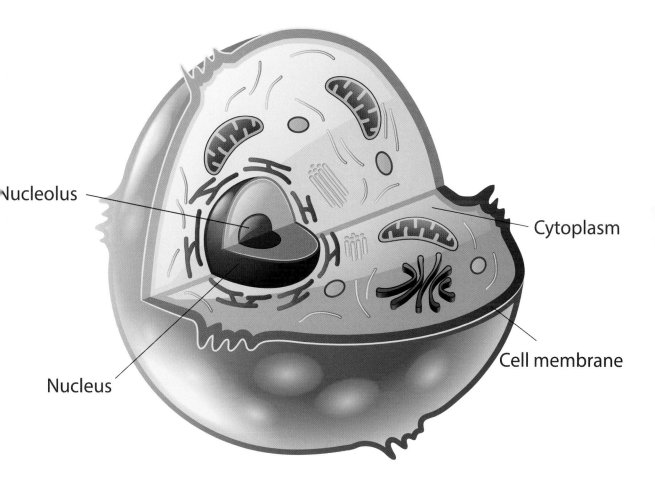

The role of cytoplasm is to give a cell its shape. It helps fill out the cell and keeps organelles in their place. Without cytoplasm, the cell would be deflated and materials would not be able to pass easily from one organelle to another.

Why are most cells so small?

In this experiment, you'll investigate how size affects a cell's ability to take up molecules it needs from its environment.

Materials:
- safety goggles
- a peeled, cooked potato
- food coloring (any color but yellow)
- a metric ruler
- a knife
- a small glass jar with ½ cup (125 milliliters) of warm water
- a spoon
- a paper towel

Instructions:
1. Put on the safety goggles.
2. From the potato, cut a 0.79 inch (2 cm) cube, a 0.4 inch (1 cm) cube, and a .20 inch (0.5 cm) cube. Use the ruler to measure. These cubes represent cells of different sizes. Save the rest of the potato. Have an adult help with this part of the project.
3. Add 40 drops of food coloring to the jar of water. The food coloring represents molecules that the cells need to survive.
4. Place the three cubes in the bottom of the glass jar.
5. After 20 minutes, use the spoon to remove the three cubes from the food coloring.
6. Place the cubes on the paper towel.
7. With the help of an adult, slice each potato cube in half. Compare their color to a piece of the original potato.
8. Measure how far the food coloring has traveled into each cube.

What did you find? Which cell received enough of the needed molecule (food coloring) throughout its interior to survive? What problem might the largest cell have?

Food for thought:
A cell needs to have enough cell membrane in contact with its outside environment so that nutrients or wastes can easily move into and out of the cell.

The smaller a cell is, the more cell membrane it has relative to what it holds inside. This means that it's easier for a small cell to get what it needs from its environment. A bigger cell may not be able to get enough nutrients to its center to survive.

PROKARYOTES VS. EUKARYOTES

There are two main types of cells: prokaryotes and eukaryotes. Prokaryotes are simple, small organisms, like bacteria. Most are unicellular, but some join together into groups. Prokaryotic cells have no nucleus, meaning that their DNA, which is often stored as a single circular molecule, is not held in a membrane.

Eukaryotes are more **complex** than prokaryotes. Their cells are generally a lot bigger, with volumes that are up to a thousand times greater, Eukaryotes can be unicellular like yeast or amoeba, or multicellular. Animals, plants, and fungi are all eukaryotes.

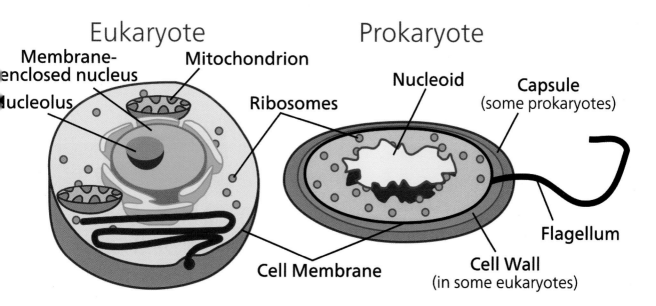

Eukaryote

Membrane-enclosed nucleus

Mitochondrion

Nucleolus

Ribosomes

Cell Membrane

Prokaryote

Nucleoid

Capsule
(some prokaryotes)

Flagellum

Cell Wall
(in some eukaryotes)

Scientists have come up with a system to classify living things. At the highest level, all organisms can be divided into one of three domains, or major branches of life: Archaea, Bacteria, and Eukaryota. All organisms in the Archaea and Bacteria domains are prokaryotes. The Eukaryota domain includes more complex, mostly multicellular forms of life, all of which are eukaryotes.

Phylogenetic Tree of Life

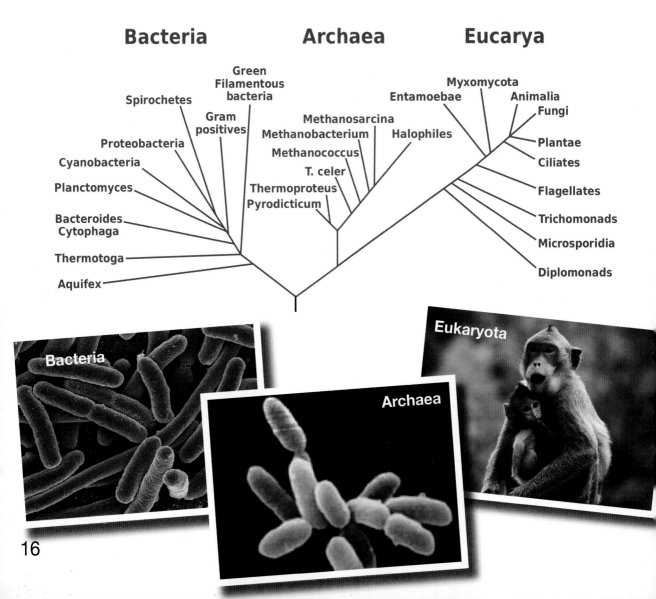

Even though we can't see bacteria and archaebacteria, these tiny organisms are everywhere. Your body contains ten times more bacterial cells than human cells! Prokaryotes are very diverse, and with somewhere between 9×10^{29} and 31×10^{29} microbes on the planet, they make up most of life on Earth.

Did You Know?

Many (but not all!) archaebacteria live in extreme environments. They've been found in boiling hot springs, super-salty pools, deep in the ocean and in Antarctic ice.

How do they do it? They make a variety of molecules and enzymes that protect them and allow them to adapt.

Grand Primatic Springs

How can you tell a prokaryotic cell from a eukaryotic cell?

One major difference is that eukaryotic cells have membrane-enclosed organelles and prokaryotes do not.

The nucleus is the most important organelle in a eukaryotic cell. It is sometimes called the cell's brain. This is where the cell's genetic information is stored in the form of DNA. Inside the nucleus, strands of DNA are packed into structures called chromosomes.

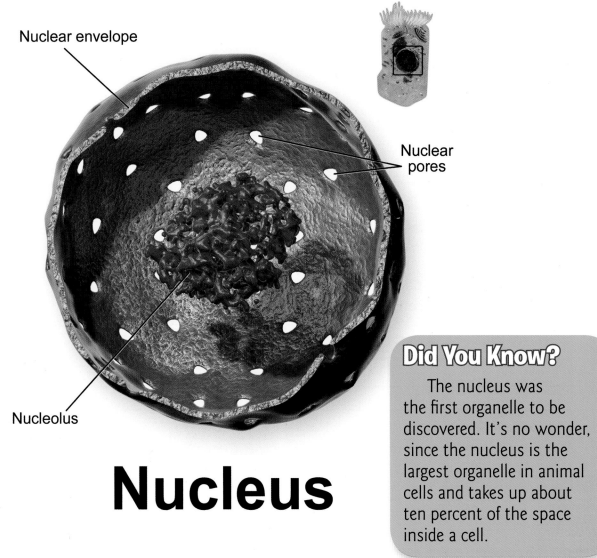

Nuclear envelope

Nuclear pores

Nucleolus

Nucleus

18

Here are some other organelles found in eukaryotic cells:

- Mitochondria have what it takes to keep a cell energized! They convert organic molecules (food) into energy the cell can use.

- Lysosomes are the garbage disposers of the cell. They get rid of wastes by breaking them down.

- Vacuoles act as storage facilities for water, food and other molecules. In plants, they help cells maintain their stiff structure.

Mitochondria on the Move

Mitochondria can change shape and move around the cell as needed. They can increase their numbers when the cell needs more energy, and can decrease or become inactive if a cell's energy needs drop.

Mitochondria are small organelles floating free throughout a cell. Some cells have several thousand mitochondria while others have none at all.

- The endoplasmic reticulum is a major manufacturing and distribution center of the cell. Some parts of this network of folded membrane are studded with protein-producing ribosomes. Proteins made in the endoplasmic reticulum are packaged and sent to the Golgi apparatus.

- The Golgi apparatus is another factory-like organelle that processes, packages and sends proteins and other molecules around the cell.

- The cytoskeleton is not an organelle, although its job is just as important. Like a skeleton or **scaffolding**, it helps the cell maintain its structure and stay organized.

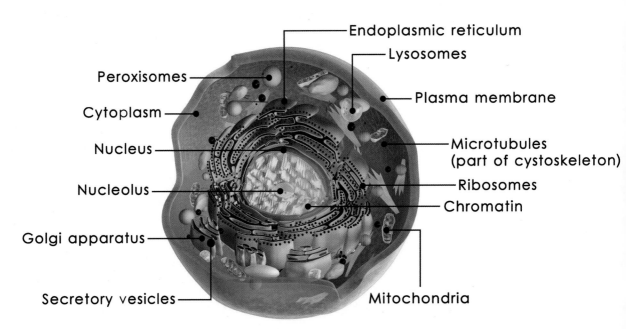

Multicellular Organisms: Getting Organized

Most eukaryotes are complex organisms with many layers of organization. When a group of similar cells works together to carry out a function needed for life, they form a tissue. For example, while one muscle cell can't make a heart pump, many working together as a tissue can.

When a group of tissues works together on the same tasks, they form an organ. A heart is an organ that is made of muscle, nerve, and blood tissues that pumps blood through the body.

When organs work together as a set, they form a system. The heart, along with veins and arteries, is part of the circulatory system.

A group of interacting systems, such as the digestive, respiratory, and skeletal muscular systems, and many others, make up a complex organism.

Your body works like a machine, with different systems, or organs, that make up your body and allow it to run effectively. Like a machine, if one system is not running properly, it could affect your whole body.

PLANT VS. ANIMAL

Plants and animals look very different from each other. But on a cellular level, they have a lot in common. Plant and animal cells are both eukaryotic. They have many organelles in common, and they can organize and work together for a common purpose.

But, as you might expect, they also have some major differences.

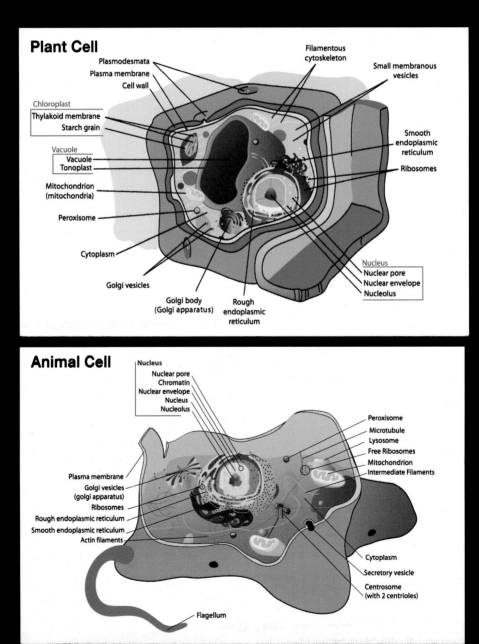

Plant cells can do one very important thing that animal cells can't: they can convert energy from the sun into food. They do this through a process called photosynthesis.

Organelles called chloroplasts are the sites where photosynthesis happens.

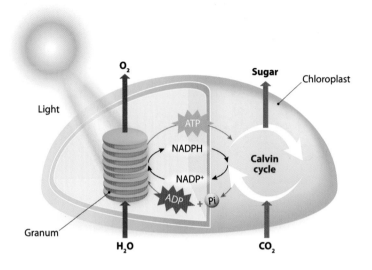

PROCESS OF PHOTOSYNTHESIS

Life on Earth is based on plants' abilities to make energy-rich food. Plants use this food themselves, and also pass it on to the organisms that eat them. Without plants, there would be no web of life as we know it.

Fast Chloroplast Facts

- A plant cell can have one or two chloroplasts, or hundreds.
- Chloroplasts give plants their green color.
- They can move around inside a cell to get the most sun exposure.
- Each chloroplast contains its own DNA and ribosomes.

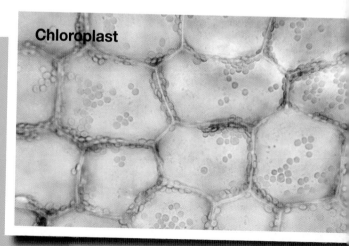

Chloroplast

Most chloroplasts are oval-shaped blobs, but they can come in all sorts of shapes such as cups, stars, or ribbons.

23

Plant cells are surrounded by strong, rigid cell walls. These walls protect the cells and give them their boxy shape. They also provide support for tall, upright structures like stalks and tree trunks.

If a cell without a cell wall is like a water balloon, then a cell with a cell wall would be like a water balloon packed snugly inside a cardboard box. Which would be easier to stack as high as a sunflower? Or a maple tree?

Dehydrated = Droopy

Plants store water and nutrients in organelles called vacuoles. At times, a vacuole can fill up to 90 percent of the space inside a cell. Vacuoles help control the size and stiffness of a cell. When you see a droopy or wilting plant, chances are that its vacuoles have shrunk due to a lack of water.

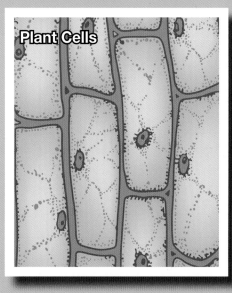

Plant Cells

Plant cells are unique. You can find three different features: chloroplast, nucleus, and a vacuole.

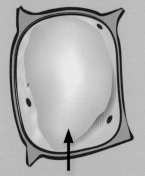

hydrated vacuole

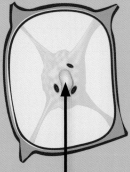

dehydrated vacuole

Multicellular plants are organized into two main organ systems: roots and shoots.

Roots grow underground and contain organs that store food and take water and dissolved minerals up from the soil.

Shoots include organs such as stems, leaves, and flowers.

- Leaves are the main sites for photosynthesis.
- Stems transport food, water, and minerals throughout the plant and provide structural support for leaves and flowers.
- Flowers, fruits, and seeds are involved in plant reproduction.

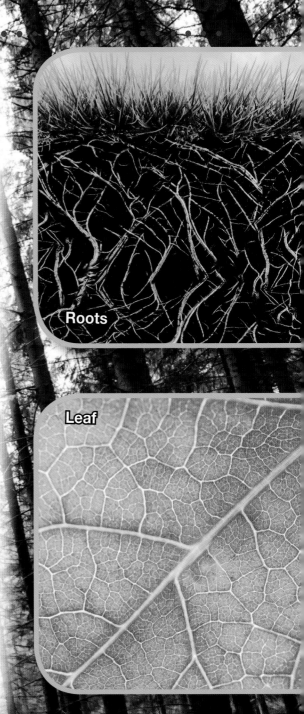

Roots

Leaf

Animal cells differ from plant cells in several ways. Animal cells have no cell wall. Instead of being boxy in shape, they tend to be spherical.

Animals do not harness energy with chloroplasts. Instead they get their energy from the food they eat. Animal cells have organelles called mitochondria (plants have these too), which break down food molecules to make chemical energy.

Swallowed Up

Many scientists believe that mitochondria were once free-living bacteria. When a more complex cell swallowed one of these bacteria, the bacteria kept right on living inside that cell. The two cells helped each other survive and over time, the bacteria lost its ability to live on its own and became an organelle. Chloroplasts are also thought to have started out as free-living bacteria. Both of these organelles contain their own genetic information separate from what's in the nucleus, and can make copies of themselves.

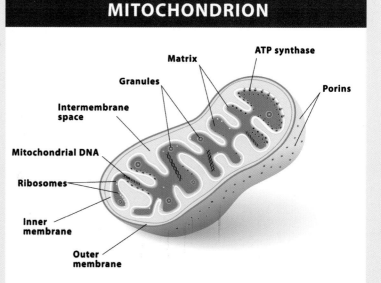

MITOCHONDRION

ATP synthase

Matrix

Granules

Porins

Intermembrane space

Mitochondrial DNA

Ribosomes

Inner membrane

Outer membrane

What about fungi? These important and often overlooked eukaryotes are not plants or animals. They are unique enough to be classified in their own Kingdom.

Like plants, fungi have stiff cell walls. But the walls are made of different materials.

Like animals, fungi can't make their own food. Instead, they get it by eating organic matter. Fungi are decomposers—they break down dead or decaying organisms, and recycle the nutrients so that other organisms can use them. This gives them a critical role in the web of life.

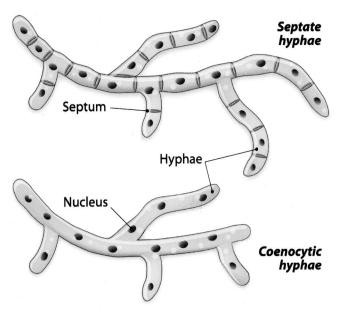

FUNGI

Septate hyphae

Septum

Hyphae

Nucleus

Coenocytic hyphae

BUILDING WITH CELLS/ CELL DIVISION

Every minute, cells in your body die—but you keep right on living! How is this possible?

Cells are constantly making more of themselves. They do this through a process called cell division.

New cells can replace dead ones and repair damage. When they increase the overall number of cells in an organism, they cause it to grow.

That's Life

Trillions of cell divisions occur in the human body every day!

Approximate cell life spans:
- white blood cells can be as short as a few days
- outer skin cells: 14 to 30 days
- red blood cells:120 days
- liver cells: 300 to 500 days
- muscle cells: 25 years on average
- nerve cell: a lifetime

There are three main ways for a cell to divide: binary fission, mitosis, and meiosis.

Prokaryotes divide by binary fission. A cell makes a second copy of its DNA and grows until it has doubled in size. Then it spits in two, with one copy of DNA in each new cell.

Eukaryotes make new cells by mitosis or meiosis.

There are two types of cell division: mitosis and meiosis. Usually when people refer to cell division they mean mitosis, the process of making new body cells. Meiosis is the type of cell division that creates egg and sperm cells.

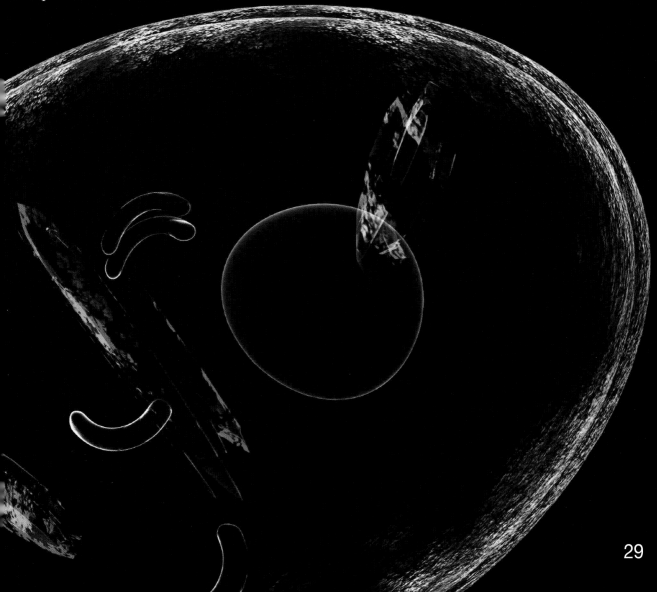

Cell Division by Mitosis

Like binary fission, mitosis starts with one cell and ends with two cells that are exact copies of each other. But because eukaryotic cells are more complicated and have more parts, they take more steps to divide.

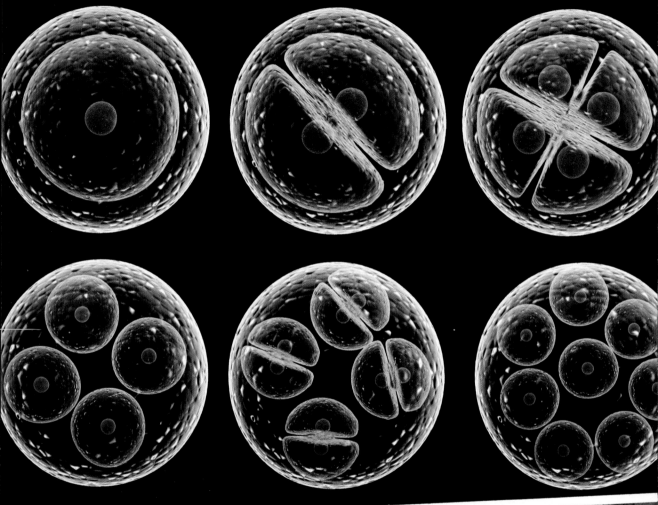

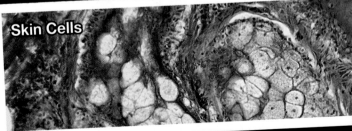

Skin Cells

Skin is the largest organ in our bodies. It has three main layers, the epidermis, the dermis, and the subcutaneous layer.

The Steps of Mitosis

In a typical animal cell, mitosis can be divided into stages:

1. Prophase: The cell gets ready to divide. Its DNA packs tightly into chromosomes, and the membrane around the nucleus breaks down.

2. Metaphase: All of the chromosomes line up along the midline of the cell.

3. Anaphase: Separation begins! Identical copies of each chromosome move to opposite sides of the cell.

4. Telophase: A nuclear membrane forms around each of the two sets of DNA. The cell then splits down the middle to create two new cells, each with a complete set of genetic information.

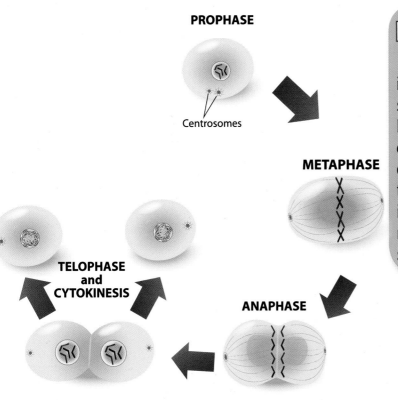

PROPHASE

Centrosomes

METAPHASE

ANAPHASE

TELOPHASE and CYTOKINESIS

It's a Cell's Life

What about when a cell isn't dividing? Its normal state is called interphase. During interphase, a cell carries out all its ordinary day-to-day tasks. This is also the time when it duplicates its DNA, so that it will be ready the next time it gets a signal to divide.

Activity: Mitosis Magic

Make a cell divide on paper with a cell cycle flip book. Then watch mitosis happen right before your eyes!

Materials:
- 12 index cards (a pad of Post-it notes with at least 12 sheets also works well)
- stapler with staples
- colored pencils
- cell cycle diagram

Instructions:
- Find a good reference picture showing the stages of mitosis. You can use the picture on page 31 or find another one online or in a cell biology textbook.
- Use one of the index cards to make a title page.
- Draw each phase of mitosis on separate cards, using at least two cards for each phase. Position the drawings toward the right-hand side of each card, and make all of the cells about the same size. You should have:
    - Prophase - 2 cards
    - Metaphase - 2 cards
    - Anaphase - 2 cards
    - Telophase - 2 cards
- Add cards for
    - Interphase —2 cards
- Color your drawings, using the same colors for the same cell parts throughout.
- Stagger your cards ever so slightly. This will make it easier to flip your book.
- Staple your book down the left side.

- Flip the pages to see mitosis in animated action!

Cell Division by Meiosis

Meiosis is a special kind of cell division used by multicellular organisms for sexual reproduction. In meiosis, one cell divides into four new cells. Each new cell has half the DNA of the original cell. Eggs and sperms are cells that are produced by meiosis.

When an egg and a sperm cell join together, they form a single fertilized egg cell with DNA from both parents. This cell will give rise to a new and unique organism.

Diploids and Haploids

The cells produced from mitosis are called diploids because they have two complete sets of chromosomes. People have two copies of most genes, one copy inherited from each parent.

The cells produced from meiosis are called haploids because they have only half the number of chromosomes as the original cell.

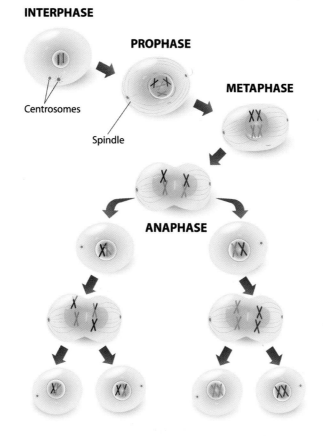

INTERPHASE

PROPHASE

METAPHASE

Centrosomes

Spindle

ANAPHASE

If cells are always made from other cells, where did the first cells come from?

No one knows how life on Earth began, but there is fossil evidence that prokaryotic cells existed 3.8 billion years ago.

Scientists have wondered if early conditions on Earth could have given rise to life. They've done experiments to show that nonliving molecules could have come together to eventually form living cells.

Stem cells are a special type of cell with a unique ability: when they divide, they can make more stem cells, or become a specialized cell, such as a muscle cell, a red blood cell, or a brain cell.

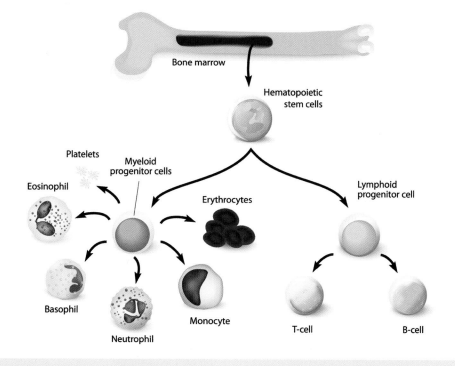

Small and Mighty

Stem cells play a critical role in our development. New life starts out as one cell, then divides into two, then four, then eight cells, and so on. As stem cells in a developing organism divide, they develop into specialized cells that form various tissues and organs.

A fully developed organism has adult stem cells in some areas of the body such as bone marrow, the liver, and the brain. These cells can divide to replace specialized cells that have worn or have been damaged by injury or disease.

Scientists are interested in using stem cells to treat diseases such as cancer.

BUILDING YOU

You are 100 percent made of cells. Your body has about 210 different types of cells. Each type does a different job to help your body function. The cells are arranged so that they can work together to make a living organism—you!

How do your cells know what to do? A cell's activities are directed by their DNA. Even though they don't all look or act alike, each one of your 37 trillion cells contains the same genetic information, in the form of DNA. This DNA directs everything that happens inside your body, telling each cell what it needs to do to help keep you alive.

Wrong Instructions!

Sometimes there are mistakes in a person's DNA. These mistakes can happen when DNA is being copied during cell division. They can also be caused by something in the environment, or be inherited from a parent.

Mistakes in DNA can cause certain cells to get the wrong instructions. One mistake that can be passed from parent to child causes red blood cells, which carry oxygen throughout the body, to have a crescent shape instead of a normal disk shape. These crescent-shaped cells can't do their job properly, and cause a disease called sickle cell anemia.

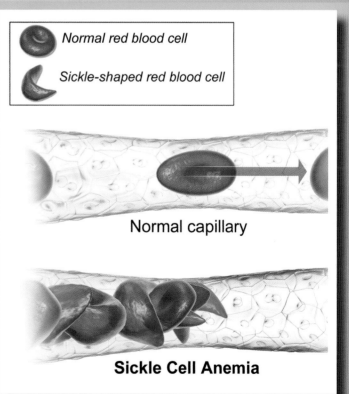

Normal red blood cell

Sickle-shaped red blood cell

Normal capillary

Sickle Cell Anemia

Cell Talk

Cells can use chemical signals to communicate with each other, share information, and coordinate activities. Cellular communication is very complicated, and many scientists spend their entire careers studying just one small part of it.

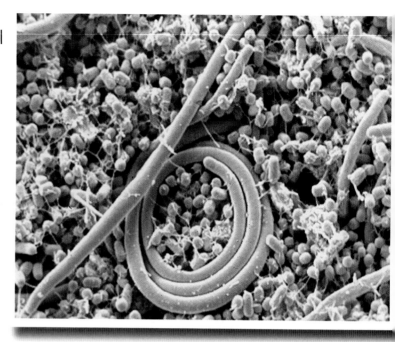

The study of cell communication focuses primarily on how a cell gives and receives messages with its environment and with itself.

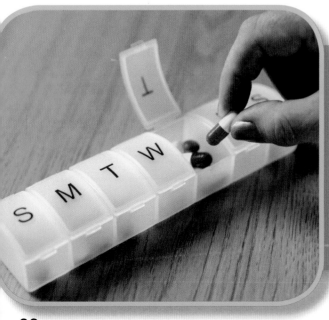

Message in a Bottle

Most medicines that we take work by giving cells a chemical message to change or stop certain activities. When we take medicine, we are changing some of the conversations going on inside our bodies.

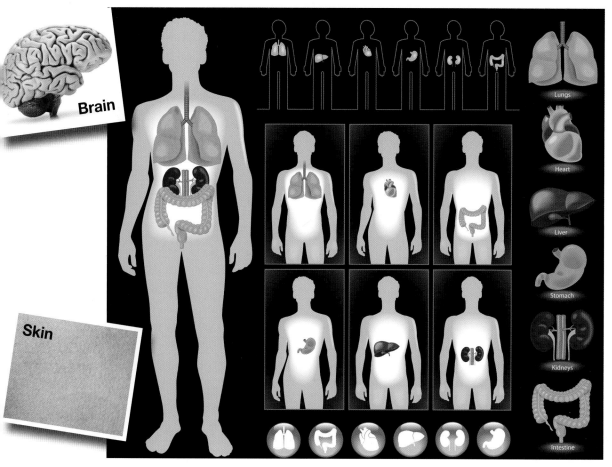

Organs Galore!

We know that cells combine into tissues, which combine to form organs. Here are just a few of the organs in your body that work together to keep you alive. Can you think of more?

- Our brain controls the rest of our body. It allows us to think and to feel emotions.
- The lungs deliver oxygen into our blood stream.
- The liver does many important things, including getting rid of toxins in the body.
- The kidneys also help clean toxins and other wastes from our bodies.
- The stomach helps break down food.
- The skin covers and protects our body from the environment.
- The heart pumps oxygen and nutrients throughout the body.

39

Organ Systems

Organs group together to form organ systems that are responsible for certain functions. For example, our immune systems, which include the spleen, lymph nodes, thymus, and bone marrow, protect us from bacterial and viral invaders.

System Name	What It Includes	What It Does
respiratory system	lungs, larynx, and airways	allows us to breathe
cardiovascular system	heart, blood, and blood vessels	carries blood and nutrients throughout the body
digestive system	stomach, gallbladder, intestines, liver, and pancreas	breaks food into molecules that can be used by different parts of the body
excretory system	kidneys and bladder	kelps your body to get rid of toxins
integumentary system	skin, hair, and nails	protects the body from the outside world
muscular system	all the muscles in our bodies	protects the body from the outside world
nervous system	brain, spinal cord, and nerves	relays messages between the brain and various parts of the body

When you think about it, it's amazing that cells can come together to form systems as complicated as ourselves.

Sometimes, though, things can go wrong. Take cancer, for example. Cancer is any disease caused by cells that keep dividing when they shouldn't. These uncontrolled cells form tumors. They slowly destroy good cells, and can lead to sickness or even death.

Cancer Cell

Curing Cancer

Cancer can often be treated and even cured. Surgery can physically remove the cancer cells, chemotherapy uses chemicals to destroy them, and radiation uses high-energy waves to do the same.

Growing Cells in a Lab

Scientists have figured out ways to grow cells in an artificial environment. This is called cell or tissue culture. It's an important tool for studying cells from multicellular organisms, without having live animals in the lab.

Microfluidic devices for stem cell cultivation and proliferation

Frankenmeat?!

Some researchers are experimenting with growing tissue as a source of edible meat! Some pluses: No animals are harmed and it could be less harmful to the environment than raising animals for meat. Some negatives: it's expensive and some people view it as creepy and unnatural. Lab-grown meat has even been given some interesting nicknames, like "Shmeat" and "Frankenmeat"!

In London in 2013, food critics tasted the very first hamburger made from billions of cow tissue culture cells and liked it!

TOOLS OF THE CELL TRADE

Most cells are too small for us to see with our eyes. Human eyes can see down to about 100 **micrometers**. A human egg is about this size, but most animal's cells are only 10 to 20 micrometers. Bacteria and mitochondria are about 0.5 micrometers in size.

Enter the microscope! A standard light microscope can help you see things as small as 0.2 micrometers. To see even tinier objects, like the details of a cell membrane or organelle, there are electron microscopes. They use beams of electrons instead of light and can reveal objects as small as 0.00005 micrometers.

Light Microscopes	Electron Microscopes
use visible light	use a beam of electrons
magnification is limited	have higher magnification
allow you to easily observe most cells	some can resolve viruses, which are far smaller than any cell
cells can be alive or dead, stained or not stained	cells have to be prepared in a way that kills them
inexpensive	expensive
easy to use	require training to use
small and portable	large and stationary

In 2014, the Nobel Prize in chemistry was awarded to three scientists—Eric Betzig, Stefan W. Hell, and William E. Moerner—for developing ways to see living cells at a much smaller scale than ever before.

Their new **microscopy** methods cause parts of cells to light up. This allows scientists to see what is happening to individual molecules inside living cells, in real time!

As these and other new tools and techniques for studying cells are developed, scientists will continue to make groundbreaking discoveries about cells and how they work. Cell biology is an exciting field of study. After all, without these fascinating and amazing mini-machines, there would be no life on Earth as we know it!

Eric Betzig

Stefan W. Hell

William E. Moerner

Super-Resolved Fluorescence Microscopy

How does this new type of microscopy, called super-resolved fluorescence microscopy, work? Here's a simple way to think about it: if light microscopy is like using a giant searchlight to spot a tiny object in a large field, then this new type is like adding tiny lights to the object itself, so that it stands out from the rest of the field.

Timeline of Early Cell Discoveries

Robert Hooke
1635–1703

1655 Robert Hooke discovers cells while looking at cork (dead plant material) through a microscope. He gives them their name.

Anton van Leeuwenhoek
1633–1732

1674 Anton van Leeuwenhoek sees living cells (protozoa). Several years later, he discovers bacteria.

1833 Robert Brown observes and describes the nucleus in plant cells.

Matthias Schleiden
1804–1881

1838 Matthias Schleiden introduces the idea that all plants are made of cells.

1839 Theodor Scwhann states that all animals are made of cells.

Albrecht von Roelliker
1818–1902

1840 Albrecht von Roelliker realizes that sperm and eggs are types of cells.

1845 Carl Heinrich Braun states that cells are the basic unit of life.

Rudolph Virchow
1821–1902

1858 Rudolph Virchow states that cells only develop from existing cells.

So You Wanna Be a Cell Sleuth

If you think you'd like to become a cell biologist, you can get started today. Use a magnifying glass to look for tiny signs of life. If you have access to a microscope, examine water from a pond or puddle.
Find out if there are any labs that study cells in your area, and see if you can schedule a visit or ask your teacher to organize a field trip.

GLOSSARY

complex (KAHM-pleks): very complicated, not simple

diversity (di-VUR-si-tee): variety

energy (EN-ur-jee): usable power

functions (FUHNGK-shuhns): special roles, activities or purposes

gene (jeen): a portion of DNA that affects the way a living thing looks, grows, and/or acts

genetic information (juh-NET-ik in-fur-MAY-shuhn): knowledge or facts having to do with genes

microbes (MYE-krobes): extremely small living things

micrometers (mye-KROH-me-tuhrz): measurement that equals one millionth of a meter

microscopy (mye-KROH-skoh-pee): the use of a microscope

nutrients (NOO-tree-uhnts): substances that living things need to live, grow and be healthy

organism (OR-guh-niz-uhm): a living thing

photosynthesis (foh-toh-SIN-thi-sis): a chemical process by which green plants turn water and carbon dioxide into food using energy from the sun

proteins (PROH-teens): chemical compounds needed for life

reproduce (ree-pruh-DOOS): to produce new individuals of the same kind

scaffolding (SKAF-uhld-ing): supporting framework

INDEX

diversity 6

DNA 9, 10, 11, 12, 15, 18, 23, 29, 31, 33, 36, 37

energy 4, 8, 19, 23, 26, 41

eukaryote(s) 15, 16, 21, 27, 29

gene 10, 33

microbes 4, 17

microscopy 44

nutrients 7, 14, 24, 27, 39, 40

organ(s) 12, 21, 25, 35, 39, 40

organelle(s) 12, 18, 19, 20, 22, 24, 26, 43

prokaryote(s) 15, 16, 17, 18, 29

protein(s) 10, 11, 12, 13, 20

reproduce 4, 7, 8

system(s) 16, 21, 25, 40, 41

SHOW WHAT YOU KNOW

1. How are prokaryotes and eukaryotes different?
2. Name four organelles and what they do.
3. What are some of the levels of organization inside your body?
4. How do cells know what to do?
5. What can the shape and size of a cell tell us about it? Give an example.

WEBSITES TO VISIT

www.exploratorium.edu/traits/exhibits.html

www.sheppardsoftware.com/health/anatomy/cell/index.htm

www.centreofthecell.org/learn-play/games

About the Author

Jodie Mangor spent years researching the mysterious inner workings of cells. These days, she puts her degrees in microbiology, environmental science, and molecular biology to work by editing papers for publication in scientific journals. Her stories, poems, and articles have appeared in a variety of children's magazines, and she has authored audio tour scripts for high-profile museums and tourist destinations around the world. Many of these tours are for kids. She lives in Ithaca, New York, with her family.

Meet The Author!
www.meetREMauthors.com

www.rourkeeducationalmedia.com

PHOTO CREDITS: Cover/Title Page © paulista - Shutterstock; Page 6 © Darrin Henry; Page 8 © Aldo Ottaviani; Psge 11 © somersault1824; Page 13 © andegro4ka; Page 15, 16, 17 © wiki; Page 17 © Henrik5000; Page 18, 37 © BruceBlaus; Psge 19 © ugreen; Page 20 © 7activestudio; Page 21 © angelhell; Page 23 © Nancy Nehring; Page 24 © Katarina Gondova, daseugen; Page 25 © andreusk, aleksle; Page 26 © gutang; Page 27 © DebraLee Wiseberg, Zhabska T.; Page 28 © Christian Anthony; Page 30 © Lukiyanova Natalia, Karl Dolenc; Page 31 © BeholdingEye; Page 32, 35 © Zhabska T.; Page 34 © Krasstin; Page 36 © Jean-Phillipe WALLET; Page 38 © USDA, wragg; Page 39 DNY59, Bukkerka; Page 41 © Jezperklauzen, KatarzynaBialasiewicz; Page 42 © The Crimson Monkey; Page 43 © Onur Döngel; Page 44 © barcande-jeremy, Kevin Lowder; Page 45 © Jan Verkolje

Edited by: Keli Sipperley

Cover design by: Nicola Stratford   www.nicolastratford.com
Interior design by: Rhea Magaro

Library of Congress PCN Data

Cells: Constructing Living Things / Jodie Mangor
(Let's Explore Science)
ISBN 978-1-68191-397-1 (hard cover)
ISBN 978-1-68191-439-8 (soft cover)
ISBN 978-1-68191-478-7 (e-Book)
Library of Congress Control Number: 2015951564

Also Available as:

MUSEUM **123**

Little, Brown and Company

Time Warner Book Group
1271 Avenue of the Americas, New York, NY 10020
Visit our Web site at www.lb-kids.com

Work by Thomas Hart Benton © T. H. Benton and R. P. Benton
Testamentary Trusts/UMB Bank Trustee/Licensed by VAGA, New York.
Work by Stuart Davis © Estate of Stuart Davis/Licensed by VAGA, New York.
Work by Alma Lavenson © Alma Lavenson Associates.

First Edition: October 2004

10 9 8 7 6 5 4 3 2

Printed in China

Produced by the Department of Special Publications,
The Metropolitan Museum of Art:
Robie Rogge, Publishing Manager; Jessica Schulte, Project Editor;
Anna Raff, Designer; Mahin Kooros, Production Associate.
All photography by The Metropolitan Museum of Art Photograph Studio.

Library of Congress Cataloging-in-Publication Data

Museum 123 / by the Metropolitan Museum of Art.— 1st ed.
    p. cm.
    ISBN 0-316-16044-X (Little, Brown and Company)
    ISBN 1-58839-118-3 (The Metropolitan Museum of Art)
    1. Counting—Juvenile literature. I. Title: Museum one two
three. II. Series: Metropolitan Museum of Art (New York, N.Y.)
QA113.M885 2004
513.2'11—dc22

                                                    2004004583

MUSEUM 123

THE METROPOLITAN MUSEUM OF ART • New York

LITTLE, BROWN AND COMPANY

New York ∾ Boston

How many

unicorns

rest in the garden?

ONE

How many

elephants

are charging?

TWO

How many

red buses

rush through busy city streets?

3

THREE

How many

kittens

follow their mother?

FOUR

How many

trapeze artists

perform for the crowd?

FIVE

How many

berries

tempt the squirrel?

6

SIX

How many men wear  colorful sashes around their waists?

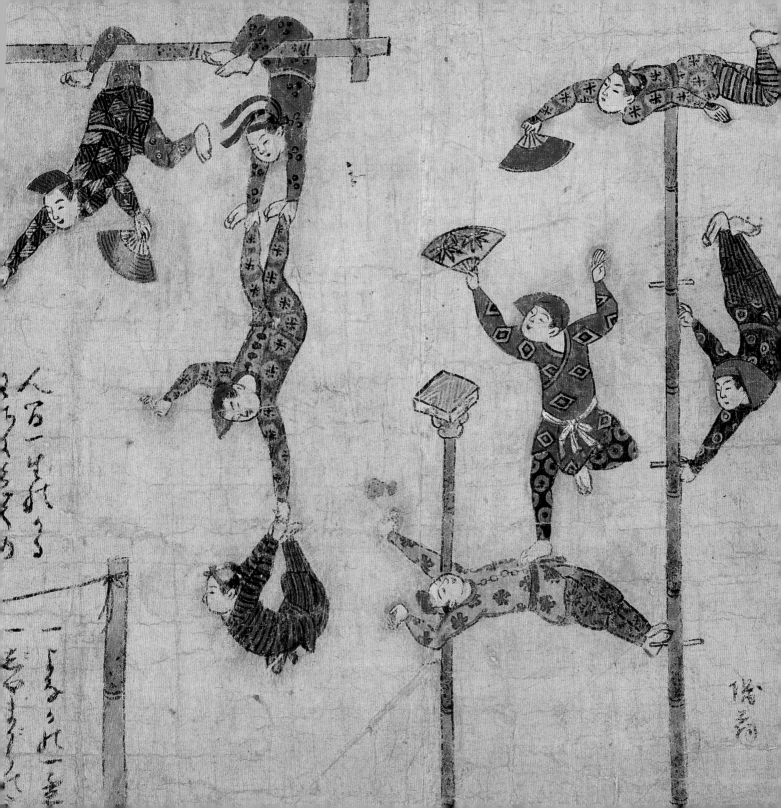

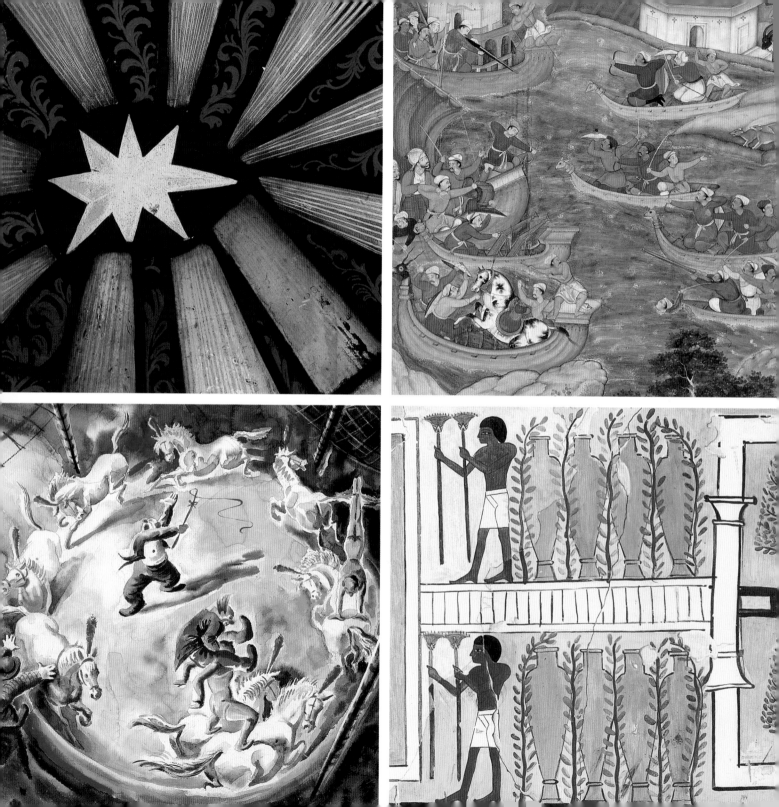

SEVEN

How many  dangle and balance?

NINE

How many

buttons

decorate this fancy uniform?

10

TEN

The captions correspond to the pictures at the top of each column, reading clockwise from top left.

1

The Unicorn in Captivity (detail)
Tapestry from the series *The Hunt of the Unicorn as Lover*
Southern Netherlands, 1495–1505
Wool warp; wool, silk, silver, and gilt wefts,
12 ft. 1 in. x 8 ft. 3 in.
Gift of John. D. Rockefeller Jr., 1937   37.80.6

Camel (detail)
Spain, from the Church of San Baudelio de
Berlanga, ca. 1120–40
Fresco, 96 x 53½ in.
The Cloisters Collection, 1961   61.219

Paris en Ballon (detail)
James Arnout, French, 1814–1868
Hand-colored lithograph, 11 x 17 in., 1846
Gift of Paul Bird Jr., 1962   62.696.2

Rank Badge with Peacock (detail)
Chinese, Qing dynasty, 1644–1911
Silk, gold- and silver-wrapped silk threads,
11½ x 11⅞ in., late 19th century
Bequest of William Christian Paul, 1929
30.75.1019

Margot in Orange Dress (detail)
Mary Cassatt, American, 1844–1926
Pastel on wove paper, mounted on canvas,
28½ x 23¾ in., 1902
From the Collection of James Stillman, Gift of
Dr. Ernest G. Stillman, 1922   22.16.25

2

*The Emperor Shah Jahan Watching
an Elephant Fight* (detail)
Bulaqi, Indian, Mughal period
Leaf from the dispersed *Padshah-Nama*
(*History of the Emperor, Shah Jahan*); ink, color,
and gold on paper, 15 x 9¾ in., ca. 1639
Harris Brisbane Dick, Louis V. Bell, Pfeiffer,
and Dodge Funds, 1989   1989.135

Detail of the coffin of Khnumnakhte
Egyptian, 12th Dynasty
Painted wood, L. 82 in.
Rogers Fund, 1915   15.2.2

The Calm Sea (detail)
Jean-Désiré-Gustave Courbet, French,
1819–1877
Oil on canvas, 23½ x 28¾ in., 1869
H. O. Havemeyer Collection, Bequest of Mrs.
H. O. Havemeyer, 1929   29.100.566

July Hay (detail)
Thomas Hart Benton, American, 1889–1975
Egg tempera, methyl cellulose, and oil on
Masonite, 38 x 26¾ in., 1943
George A. Hearn Fund, 1943   43.159.1

Dancers Practicing at the Bar (detail)
Edgar Degas, French, 1834–1917
Mixed media on canvas, 29¾ x 32 in., 1877
H. O. Havemeyer Collection, Bequest of Mrs.
H. O. Havemeyer, 1929   29.100.34

3

London Buses (detail)
Lill Tschudi, Swiss, b. 1911
Color linocut, 13⅜ x 7⁵⁄₁₆ in., 1949
Gift of Mary Ryan, 1985   1985.1060

May (detail)
Franz M. Melchers, Belgian, 1868–1944
Illustration from *L'An*, poems by Thomas Braun,
published 1897
Hand-tinted lithograph, 9¹⁵⁄₁₆ x 9¹⁵⁄₁₆ in.
The Elisha Whittelsey Collection, The Elisha
Whittelsey Fund, 1967   67.763.1

White Rooster (detail)
Milton Avery, American, 1885–1965
Oil on canvas, 61½ x 50¾ in., 1947
Gift of Joyce Blaffer von Bothmer, in memory of
Mr. and Mrs. Robert Lee Blaffer, 1975
1975.210

Flowers by a Stone Vase (detail)
Peter Faes, Flemish, 1750–1814
Oil on wood, 20 x 14⅞ in., 1786
Bequest of Catherine D. Wentworth, 1948
48.187.737

*Jean Monet (1867–1913) on His Hobby
Horse* (detail)
Claude Monet, French, 1840–1926
Oil on canvas, 23⅜ x 29¼ in., 1872
Gift of Sara Lee Corporation, 2000   2000.195

4

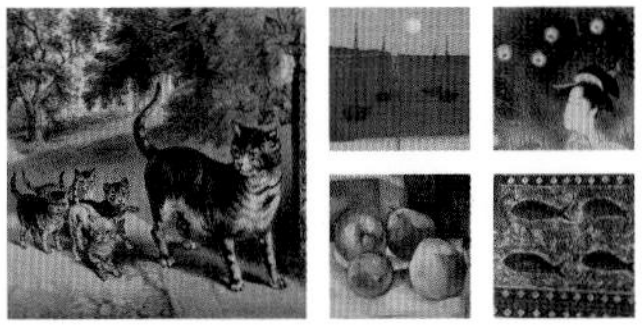

Pussy's Return (detail)
Currier and Ives (publishers), American, 1887–1907
Hand-colored lithograph, 8½ x 12½ in.
Bequest of Adele S. Colgate, 1962   63.550.314

The Skyrocket (detail)
B. J. O. Nordfeldt, American, 1878–1955
Color woodcut, 8⅝ x 11⅛ in., 1906
Gift of Mrs. B. J. O. Nordfeldt, 1955   55.634.60

Young Beauty and Child at Night Catching Fireflies (detail)
Eishosai Choki, Japanese, active ca. 1785–1805
Woodblock print, mica ground, 14 13/16 x 9⅝ in., ca. 1793
H. O. Havemeyer Collection, Bequest of Mrs. H. O. Havemeyer, 1929 JP 1739

Housepost (detail)
Yami people, Taiwan, 19th–early 20th century
Wood, paint, H. 81½ in.
From the Collection of Nina and Gordon Bunshaft, Bequest of Nina Bunshaft, 1994
1995.65.2

Still Life with Apples and Pears (detail)
Paul Cézanne, French, 1839–1906
Oil on canvas, 17⅝ x 23⅛ in., 1885–87
Bequest of Stephen C. Clark, 1960   61.101.3

5

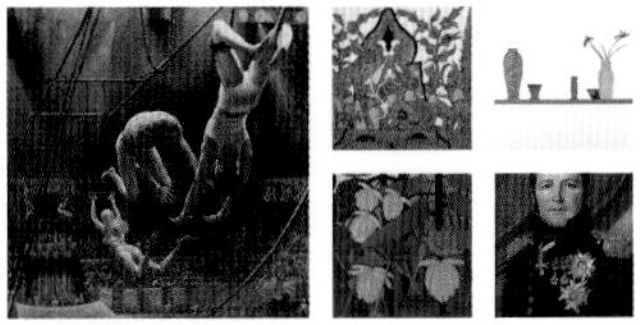

Aerial Spectacle (detail)
Mervin Honig, American, 1920–1990
Oil on canvas, 71 x 60 in., 1967
Gift of Mrs. Percy Uris, 1981   1981.32

The King of Hares in Counsel with His Subjects
Provincial Ottoman, possibly Syria, early 18th century
From *Kalila wa Dimna (The Book of the Fables of Bidpai)*
Color and ink on paper, 12 x 8⅞ in., mid-16th century
The Nasli Heeramaneck Collection, Gift of Alice Heeramaneck, 1981   1981.373, folio 66r

An American Painting—For Rose Paul (detail)
Ed Bayard, American, b. 1940
Alkyd on canvas, 48¾ x 60¼ in., 1979
Gift of Barbara and Eugene Schwartz, 1980
1980.84

General Étienne Maurice Gérard (1773–1852), Marshal of France (detail)
Jacques-Louis David, French, 1748–1825
Oil on canvas, 77⅝ x 53⅝ in., 1816
Purchase, Rogers and Fletcher Funds, and Mary Wetmore Shively Bequest, in memory of her husband, Henry L. Shively, M.D., 1965   65.14.5

The Repast of the Lion (detail)
Henri-Julien-Félix Rousseau, French, 1844–1910
Oil on canvas, 44¾ x 63 in., ca. 1907
Bequest of Sam A. Lewisohn, 1951   51.112.5

6

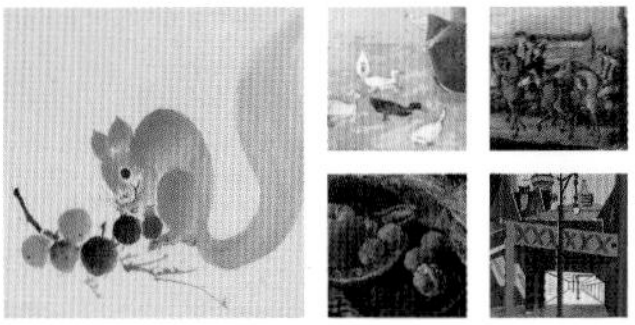

Squirrel Eating Berries (detail)
After Katsushika Hokusai, Japanese, 1760–1849
Leaf from an album of sketches by Hokusai and his disciples, 15½ x 10½ in.
Charles Stewart Smith Collection, Gift of Mrs. Charles Stewart Smith, Charles Stewart Smith Jr. and Howard Caswell Smith, in memory of Charles Stewart Smith, 1914   14.76.59.2

Feeding the Ducks (detail)
Mary Cassatt, American, 1845–1926
Drypoint, soft ground etching, and aquatint printed in color, 11 11/16 x 15¾ in., 1895
H. O. Havemeyer Collection, Bequest of Mrs. H. O. Havemeyer, 1929 29.107.100

Washington Reviewing the Western Army at Fort Cumberland, Maryland (detail)
Attributed to Frederick Kemmelmeyer, American, ca. 1755–1821
Oil on canvas, 23¾ x 37¼ in., after 1795
Gift of Edgar William and Bernice Chrysler Garbisch, 1963   63.201.2

Jefferson Market, New York (detail)
Stuart Davis, American, 1892–1964
Oil on canvas, 33⅛ x 22⅛ in., 1930
Gift of Carl D. Lobell, 1996   1996.546

Still Life with Walnuts (detail)
George Grosz, American (b. Germany), 1893–1959
Oil on canvas board, 24 x 19⅞ in., 1937
George A. Hearn Fund, 1939 39.48.2

7

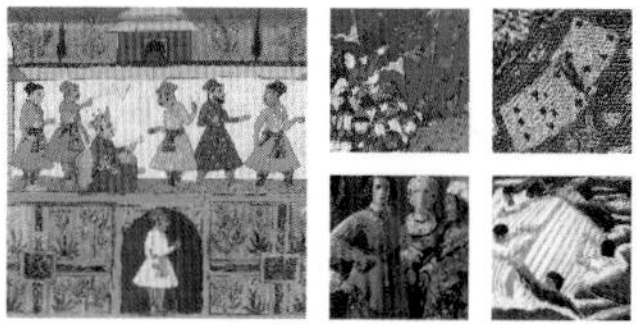

A Messenger Is Dispatched (detail)
Indian (Punjab Hills, Bilaspur), last quarter 17th century
Page from a dispersed manuscript; ink and opaque watercolor on paper, 8⅞ x 12 in.
Gift of Cynthia Hazen Polsky, 1987
1987.424.16

Zal Slays Khazarvan with the Ox-Head Mace (detail)
Attributed to Abd-al-Vahhab, Iranian (Tabriz), ca. 1525–30, with additions by Mir Susavvir
Leaf from the *Shahnama* of Shah Tahmasp; color, ink, silver, and gold on paper
Gift of Arthur A. Houghton Jr., 1970
1970.301.15

Tabletop with Trompe l'Oeil Card Game (detail)
English, 18th century
Petite and gros point embroidery in silk and wool on canvas, 31¼ x 30¾ in.
Bequest of Mrs. Annie C. Kane, 1926
26.260.49

Capsized (detail)
Richard Bosman, Australian (b. India), b. 1944
Oil on canvas, 6 x 9 ft., 1982
Gift of Mr. and Mrs. Wilson Nolen, 1983
1983.198

The Fortune Teller (detail)
Georges de La Tour, French, 1593–1652
Oil on canvas, 40⅛ x 48⅝ in., ca. 1630
Rogers Fund, 1960 60.30

8

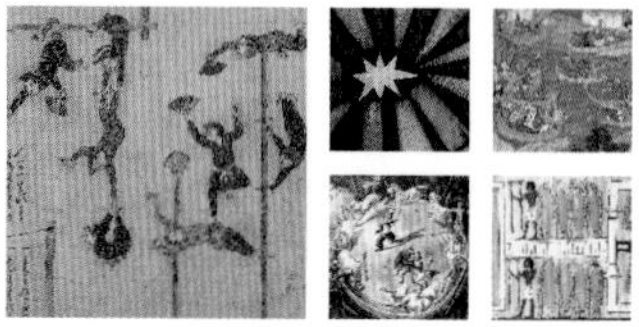

Acrobats (detail)
Japanese, Edo period
Handscroll; ink and watercolor on paper, 10 9/16 in. x 10 ft. 7⅛ in.
Gift of Mrs. Henry J. Bernheim, 1945 45.97.5

The Nativity (detail)
German, Boppard-on-the-Rhine, 1445
Stained-glass panel; pot metal, white glass, silver stain, and olive-green enamel, 43¼ x 29¼ in.
Francis L. Leland Fund, 1913 13.64.4

Alexander Fights a Sea-Battle in China (detail)
Indian, Mughal period
Leaf from a *Khamsa* (*Quintet*), by Amir Khusrav Dihlavi, 1253–1325
Ink, color, and gold on paper, 9¾ x 6¼ in., 1597–98
Gift of Alexander Smith Cochran, 1913
13.228.32

Funeral Ceremony in a Temple Garden (detail)
Egyptian, Thebes, Sheikh abd el Qurna, 18th Dynasty
Copy of a wall painting from the tomb of Minnakhte, 26¾ x 48⅛ in., ca. 1475 B.C.
Rogers Fund, 1930 30.4.56

Three Clowns in a Ring (detail)
Georges Schreiber, American, 1904–1977
Watercolor on paper, 22½ x 26¾ in., 1944
George A. Hearn Fund, 1945 45.34.6

9

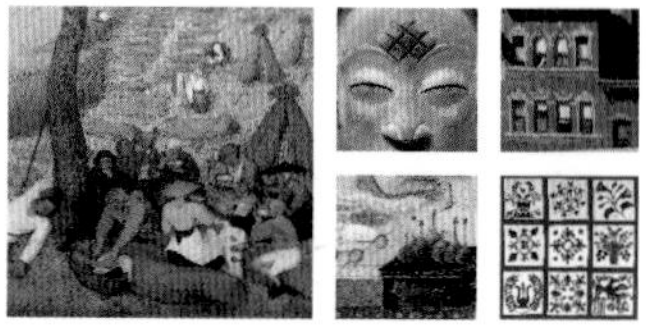

The Harvesters (detail)
Pieter Bruegel the Elder, Netherlandish, active by 1551, d. 1569
Oil on wood, 46⅞ x 63¾ in., 1565
Rogers Fund, 1919 19.164

Mukudj Dance Mask (detail)
Gabon, Punu peoples, 19th century
Wood, pigment, kaolin, L. 13½ in. x W. 7½ in. x D. 6½ in.
Purchase, Louis V. Bell Fund, and Fred and Rita Richman Foundation Gift and James J. Ross Gifts, 2000 2000.177

From Williamsburg Bridge (detail)
Edward Hopper, American, 1882–1967
Oil on canvas, 29 x 43 in., 1928
George A. Hearn Fund, 1937 37.44

Album Quilt (detail)
Brown and Turner families, American, begun in 1846
Cotton, appliquéd and quilted, 83⅜ x 85 in.
Bequest of Margaret Brown Potvin, 1987
1988.134

Princess and Attendants on a Balcony (detail)
Indian (possibly Kashmir), Mughal period
Color and gold on paper, 13⅛ x 8¼ in., late 17th century
Theodore M. Davis Collection, Bequest of Theodore M. Davis, 1915 30.95.174, folio 18

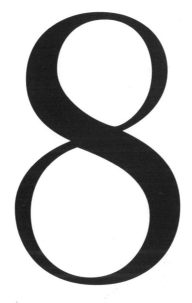

EIGHT

How many

people

relax by a tree?

10

Sergeant of the Colonial Regiment (detail)
Albert Marquet, French, 1875–1947
Oil on canvas, 35½ x 28 in.
Robert Lehman Collection, 1975   1975.1.192

The Pleasure of Fishes (detail)
Zhou Dongqing, Chinese, active late 13th century
Handscroll; ink and color on paper,
1 ft. ⅛ in x 19 ft. 5¾ in.
From the Collection of A. W. Bahr, Purchase,
Fletcher Fund, 1947   47.18.10

Hand Studies, Child with Doll (detail)
Alma Lavenson, American, 1897–1989
Platinum print, 7⁹⁄₁₆ x 9¾ in., 1932
Stewart S. MacDermott Fund, 1987   1987.1035
© Alma Lavenson Associates

Moses and Aaron Before Pharaoh: An Allegory
of the Dinteville Family (detail)
Master of the Dinteville Allegory, Netherlandish
or French, active mid–16th century
Oil on wood, 69½ x 75⅝ in., 1537
Wentworth Fund, 1950   50.70

Tables for Ladies (detail)
Edward Hopper, American, 1882–1967
Oil on canvas, 48¼ x 60¼ in., 1930
George A. Hearn Fund, 1931   31.62

trapeze artists

colorful

sashes

acrobats

red buses

buttons

people

elephants

kittens

unicorns

berries